For Mom, Dad, Greg, and Michael.
You have filled my life with love, laughter, and friendship.
And to my sis-in-laws. Erin and Amy. I love you!

A special thanks to an incredible editor.
Lois, you're the best!

THE VERY SCARY CAVE
published by Gold 'n' Honey Books
a division of Multnomah Publishers, Inc.
and in association with the literary agency of Dupree/Miller & Associates

© 1998 by Kari Smalley Gibson and Gary Smalley
Illustrations © 1998 by Richard Bernal
Designed by Kirk DouPonce

International Standard Book Number: 1-57673-267-3

Gold 'n' Honey is a trademark of Multnomah Publishers, Inc.,
and is registered in the U.S. Patent and Trademark Office.

Printed in the United States of America

For information:
MULTNOMAH PUBLISHERS, INC.
POST OFFICE BOX 1720
SISTERS, OREGON 97759

Library of Congress Cataloging-in-Publication Data:

Gibson, Kari Smalley.
    A very scary cave / by Kari Smalley Gibson.
        p.   cm.
    Summary: A beaver and a chipmunk wander away from their picnic and
end up in a cave where they are frightened by loud noises.
        ISBN (invalid) 1-57673-276-3 (alk. paper)
        [1. Beavers—Fiction. 2. Chipmunks—Fiction. 3. Fear—Fiction.]
    I. Title.
PZ7.G339297Ve   1998   98-3684
[E]—dc21   CIP
                                                                AC

98 99 00 01 02 03 04 — 10 9 8 7 6 5 4 3 2 1

Forest Tales

The Very Scary Cave

KARI SMALLEY GIBSON WITH GARY SMALLEY

Illustrated by
RICHARD BERNAL

GOLD 'N' HONEY • SISTERS, OREGON

Mooki gulped down his sandwich in one big MUNCH, then stuffed a juicy strawberry into his mouth. The critters were celebrating Mrs. Twizzer's birthday with a picnic in the meadow. Gregory had found the perfect spot for the party. The rest of the critters spread soft, colorful quilts on the new grass. Then they carried a huge picnic basket packed with yummy things to eat and placed it right in the center. Emmi had made a beautiful birthday cake decorated with candles and spring flowers. Suzzi added the finishing touch—a bouquet of tiny buttercups picked just as their heads peeked out into the spring sunshine.

Mooki's lunch was settling nicely when a little critter pounced on his lap. "Let's go exploring!" Gregory whispered.

Gregory was small, but he had a huge sense of adventure that sometimes got him into trouble.

"Wait! I haven't had any cake yet," Mooki mumbled through a mouthful of sweets.

"Oh, come on," said Gregory. "There will still be some left when we get back."

*M*ooki grudgingly followed his little friend off into the woods to explore. Just before they headed into the trees, Mrs. Twizzer shouted, "Boys, be careful not to get into trouble! Don't wander too far."

"Hurry!" Gregory exclaimed, paying little attention to Mrs. Twizzer's warning. "Let's go find a tree to climb. We'll find the tallest one!"

"I don't know how to climb trees," Mooki responded, "but I sure know how to chop them down."

Always in a hurry, Gregory dashed ahead. Mooki, on the other hand, stopped to bury his nose in a clump of fragrant wildflowers. *I'm so glad spring is finally here,* he thought dreamily. Having forgotten all about Gregory, Mooki jumped when his little friend squeaked with glee.

"I found something, Mooki!" hollered Gregory. "Let's look inside."

"What is it?" Mooki asked cautiously.

"It looks like a cave!" Gregory said, sputtering with excitement. "C'mon! We have to check it out."

Gregory darted inside the dark opening, but Mooki held back. Finally Mooki peeked his head around the corner, then pulled away with a little shiver. It was so dark in there! Mooki didn't like dark places, but he was embarrassed to tell his brave little friend.

"Mooki, where are you? It's really awesome in here!" Gregory called. "Don't be so poky."

Mooki took a deep breath and took one careful step into the cave. It was so dark that he could barely see Gregory at all.

"Gregory, wait!" called Mooki. "I can't see a thing."

"It's okay. Your eyes will get used to it," Gregory explained.

Mooki finally caught up with the little chipmunk. He felt much better holding on to Gregory's tiny paw. The cave's rock walls felt slippery and cold. Mooki had to watch his head in tight spots where pointy rocks hung down from the top of the cave.

"It's pretty creepy in here," said Mooki. Then came an echo: "creepy in here...creepy in here," and Mooki wished he hadn't said anything at all.

"Do you hear a swishing sound?" Gregory asked.

Suddenly cold water swirled around Mooki's feet, and he jumped.

"It's a little stream!" Gregory cried in delight. "Look! There's enough light to see sparkly rocks in the water. Let's each take one for a treasure!"

Mooki felt quite sure that they'd gone far enough when Gregory pointed to a dark passage that veered off to the right. He was pulling Mooki impatiently in that direction when suddenly the two friends heard a noise that made them stop dead in their tracks.

SNOOZ SNOOZA SNOOZ
BOOM BOOMA BOOM!!!

"Wowsy, what was that?" Mooki asked, shuddering.

"I don't know, but I sure don't like it," whispered Gregory, who was clinging to Mooki's paw with all his might. "We have to get out of here!" But both friends stood frozen in place.

"I-I-I knew we should have listened to Mrs. Twizzer!" Mooki whined.

"It's all my fault," Gregory admitted. "I never should have wandered in here so far. Listen—there it is again!"

SNOOZ SNOOZA SNOOZ
BOOM BOOMA BOOM!!!

"Gregory," Mooki whispered, "I don't remember which way to go! Do you think you can find your way out of here?"

"I don't think I can," Gregory said, sniffling.

Suddenly a tiny light illuminated the cave.

"What's that?" Mooki wondered aloud, peering hard into the darkness.

The light flickered and landed on top of Gregory's head.

"Why are you crying? What could be wrong?" whispered the dainty firefly. "Don't you know about the angel song?"

"The angel song?" the two friends asked.

*T*he little firefly began to sing.

(to be sung to the tune of "Twinkle, Twinkle, Little Star")

When I'm alone I don't need to fear.

My guardian angel is always near.

My special angel is sent from above

To watch over me with God's great love.

When I'm alone I don't need to fear.

My guardian angel is always near.

As the delicate notes faded, her tiny light blinked and twinkled off into the darkness.

$\mathcal{G}$regory and Mooki suddenly felt much better.

"You know, Gregory, you do have the best sense of direction of anybody I know," said Mooki. "And everyone says you're the bravest little critter of all."

"Well, I can sure do my best," Gregory said bravely. "Let's just keep going until we find a way out of here!"

Holding paws again, the two friends started off in what Gregory thought was the right direction.

All of a sudden Mooki tripped and landed smack on top of something soft and furry.

SNOOZ SNOOZA SN— OUCH!!!

The scary noise suddenly stopped.

"What was that?" shrieked Mooki, trying with all his might to get up. But the more he wiggled, the more tangled up he became with...whatever it was.

"Help, Gregory!" cried Mooki. "I can't get loose!"

Gregory pulled and pulled but couldn't break Mooki free.

"Hey," growled a sleepy, grumpy voice. "Who's rolling around on top of me? GRRR!"

"It-it-it's just me," squeaked Mooki. "I'm sorry, wh-whoever you are."

"Well, GET OFF!" ordered the grumpy, sleepy voice. "I was having a good dream and you ruined it."

Mooki opened his eyes and stared at the creature in surprise. He recognized that voice!

$\mathcal{I}$s—is that you, Gibby?" Mooki asked in a hoarse whisper.

"Of course it's me," the sleepy voice answered. "Who else would it be—the tooth fairy?"

Mooki snorted and stifled a giggle. Mooki and Gregory couldn't believe their eyes. The scary, furry creature Mooki had stumbled over was their friend Gibby!

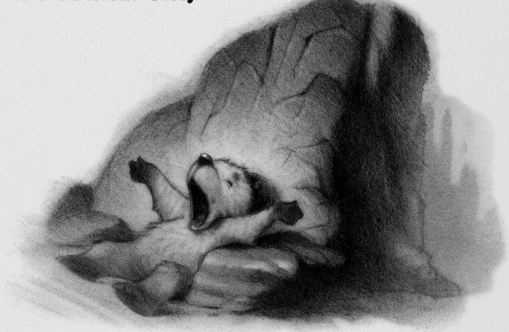

As the groggy bear cub sat up against the wall of the cave, leaves and twigs tumbled off him. Mooki and Gregory covered their mouths to keep from laughing as Gibby yawned and rubbed his sleepy eyes with his big, furry paws.

W hat are you two doing in here?" asked Gibby groggily.

"What are YOU doing in here?" Mooki and Gregory asked together.

"Hibernating," mumbled Gibby. "Or at least trying to. Don't you remember that I sleep all winter long?"

Gregory and Mooki had forgotten that Gibby slept all through the long cold winter.

"I think Mrs. Twizzer tried to get me up yesterday," Gibby explained, "but I just couldn't wake up. I was still too sleepy. Did I miss her birthday party?"

$\mathcal{W}$ell, most of it," Gregory answered. Then suddenly Mooki and Gregory started laughing so hard that they both fell over.

"What's going on?" growled the bewildered bear.

"We were scared silly," Mooki gasped through spasms of laughter.

"Right!" Gregory said between giggles. "We heard an awful noise and couldn't find our way out."

"I don't think that's very funny," said Gibby.

"It wasn't!" spouted Mooki. "But then the awful noise turned out to be...to be..."

"YOU!" Gregory had to finish the sentence because Mooki was off in whoops of laughter again.

e?" Gibby said. "Oh!" He started to giggle too. "I'm sorry I scared you. I must've been snoring."

"I'll say you were!" Gregory agreed. "We thought there must be some terrible creature in here."

"Wowsy!" replied Mooki. "How do the other critters who live here in this cave ever get any sleep?"

The three friends laughed so hard they fell back to the ground in a heap of giggles.

Suddenly Gibby sat up, his tummy rumbling. "Do you think there's any birthday cake left?" he asked.

$\mathcal{I}$f we hurry, there just might be!" Gregory squeaked.

"Gibby," Mooki asked, "can you help us find our way out of this very scary cave?"

"Be glad to," Gibby answered, "especially if there's a piece of cake out there waiting for me!"

So the beaver, the chipmunk, and the furry bear cub made their merry way out of a cave that turned out to be not so scary after all.

Gregory squinted up toward the sunny blue sky. "I'm sure glad to see the sunlight again!" he sighed.

"Gregory, from now on I think we'd better stick to climbing trees," said Mooki with a grin. "I don't think we'll find anyone snoring up in a treetop."

"Boys!" Mrs. Twizzer called. "Come over here. How nice of you to go waken Gibby so he could have some of my cake. And here I was worried that you'd wander off on some...adventure."

The three friends stuffed their mouths with cake to keep from laughing.

Small Talk

with *Gary Smalley*

Facing Fear with Courage

Parents, reading *The Very Scary Cave* with your child affords a wonderful opportunity to talk about courage. Just as Mooki and Gregory discovered that the frightening noise in the cave was nothing more than Gibby's snoring, we can help our children understand that many things that frighten them aren't so scary after all.

After you've read *The Very Scary Cave,* use the following questions to discuss fear and courage with your child:

- *What frightened Mooki and Gregory?*

- *What did the scary sound turn out to be?*

- *What gave Mooki and Gregory courage to face their fears?*

- *When is a time you felt afraid?*

- *What can help you be brave like Mooki and Gregory?*

Children may be fearful of thunderstorms, dark closets, or something they imagine to be under the bed. What's in the dark is unknown and unfamiliar. But God is there! Your encouraging attitudes and actions can help them feel safe and secure in God's love so they can move forward in the face of fear. Here are some guidelines for dealing with your child's fears.

- *Never belittle a child's fears. Fear is a very real emotion and should be understood and taken seriously.*

- *Always help the child feel safe. Leave a light on; find familiar things in a "scary" place; sing a favorite song together.*

- *Explain that God surrounds us with His love and care and that we can trust Him to take everything that happens to us and turn it into something good.*

- *Pray with the child and ask God to bring comfort.*

When my children were young and would come to me with their fears, I reminded them that nothing bad can ever happen to a child of God. I pointed out Scriptures that teach us that God uses the scary and difficult things in our lives to help us become more like Jesus. I listened to their concerns and fears and tried to help them find something good in each situation. I helped them find solutions and tried to make them feel safe. All three of my now-grown children continue to believe that the Lord works all things together for good!

Going forward and facing our fears isn't an easy thing to do, but God has given us many Scriptures to help us find our way. Here are a few verses I've looked to for guidance and shared with my children over the years: Isaiah 61:3; Romans 5:3–5; Romans 8:28; 1 Thessalonians 5:16–18; Hebrews 12:9–11; and James 1:2.

 **Kari Smalley Gibson** taught elementary school in the inner city of Phoenix, Arizona. Working with children on a daily basis, she decided to write stories that would encourage, comfort, and give hope. Kari now enjoys the slow pace of country living in Branson, Missouri, with her husband, author and speaker Roger Thomas Gibson, and their two children, Michael and Hannah Elise.

 **Richard Bernal**'s interest in art began at a young age, when he expressed himself on the chalkboard and desktop. He is now a freelance illustrator who has created illustrations for several children's books, including *Night Zoo* and the award-winning *The Ants Go Marching*. He continues to take art classes to broaden his education, and he often speaks about his work to elementary school children, which he finds an education in itself. He lives in St. Louis, Missouri.